T0095854

The Heart of Christmas

An Invitation to the Wonder of the Season

SUSAN FLORENCE

Bristol Park Books

First Bristol Park Books edition published in 2018

Bristol Park Books
252 West 38th Street
New York, NY 10018

Bristol Park Books is a registered trademark
of Bristol Park Books, Inc.

Library of Congress Control Number: 2018943107

ISBN:978-0-88486-689-3

E-Book ISBN: 978-0-88486-690-9

Text and cover design by Keira McGuinness
Cover art copyright © 2018 ZoZo design/Shutterstock

Printed in Malaysia

To:

_____

From:

_____

December dawns...
the days shorten,
the golden leaves have fallen,
and a chill is in the air.

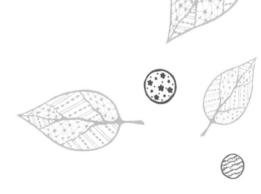

We open an invitation
to the wonder of the season
and light a lantern for Christmas,
seeking its warm and loving heart.

We take time to reflect on
the spirit of living and the
things that brings us joy—

time to

rekindle

what brings

meaning

and hope

into

our

lives,

time to prepare for the birth

of love in our hearts.

We hang wreaths of nature's greenery

as a sign of welcome,

opening our homes and hearts

to renewed life and love.

For young and old alike

the carols of Christmas

bring music to our souls.

Favorite family recipes

fill the home with scents of spices

and the promise of festive

times we will share.

We are all children as
we gaze in wonder
and delight on
the glowing
Christmas
tree.

Each ornament, so carefully
placed, shines in the light
of its own special
meaning.

We read and reflect again

on the simple story

of the first Christmas,

when Mary and Joseph

traveled far from home

and could find no

place to stay.

It was a time of birth

when security and the comfort

of home are needed more

than at any other time—

but there were no rooms in town,

only a stable.

And it was here,

in this humble dwelling

for animals,

that the Christ Child

was born.

That night a wondrous star shone in the heavens calling shepherds from their fields and Kings from distant lands.

Together, the shepherds and Kings
looked upon the infant
with wonder and joy.

Instead of trumpets,

there was silence;

and as the

Christ Child slept

love and hope

entered the

world.

We are reminded once again
that the love brought to the world
by the Christ Child
is needed now in each
of our hearts.

And the radiant star of peace
that shone in the heavens that night
needs to shine now, even brighter,
on our world.

The heart of Christmas

holds a special meaning

for each of us...

it not only feeds

the spirit,

it nurtures

the soul.

For as much

as Christmas

is many voices

singing,

so too is

Christmas

one silent

prayer for

peace.

And as much as Christmas

is a bright display of lights,

so too is Christmas

the gentle glow

of one candle

burning.

And as much as Christmas

is giving and receiving gifts,

so too is Christmas

acknowledging the gifts

we already have —

love, joy, beauty,

family, friends—life.

On Christmas we remember

the special people who

touch our lives.

Yet it is also a time

to offer loving kindness

to people we may not know,

people whose lives we can touch...

strangers who receive our smile,

meals we serve to the poor,

donations we make to others

less fortunate than we may be.

This heart of Christmas

brings us all together

to celebrate, to sing, to feel joy...

but it is also a simple time

to be quiet and alone.

It may be a time to pause

and hold dear memories

of past Christmases

with loved ones no longer here.

58

It may be a time to wake early

with fresh coffee or tea at your table,

to look out at white snowfields that

cover the farmlands where you live,

and feel the gift of the first pink blush

of sky lifting dawn into day.

Like the grace of morning light

entering the world silently

comes this deep message

of the season.

Look within this warm heart

  of Christmas.

Receive its love and feel its light

entering your heart and

illuminating your life.

Illustration Credits